John Thompson's Modern Course for the Piano   **FIRST GRADE**

CLASSICAL PIANO SOLOS

20 Original Keyboard Pieces from Baroque to Early 20th Century

COMPILED AND EDITED BY

Philip Low, Sonya Schumann, and Charmaine Siagian

T0084256

ISBN 978-1-4803-4491-4

WILLIS MUSIC

EXCLUSIVELY DISTRIBUTED BY

HAL•LEONARD®
CORPORATION

7777 W. BLUEMOUND RD. P.O. BOX 13819 MILWAUKEE, WI 53213

Visit Hal Leonard Online at
www.halleonard.com

PREFACE

A rarity among piano methods, John Thompson's *Modern Course* was authored by a successful concert artist. For this reason, the pianism found between the pages of the famous "red cover" series corresponds directly with that which is required to play authentic piano literature. A musician of the highest caliber, Thompson (1889–1963) made expert repertoire choices, integrating strong original compositions with accessible arrangements of orchestral and piano classics that perfectly represented the style characteristics of each era, resulting in well-rounded students who could approach any new piece with confidence.

The aim of the *Classical Piano Solos* series is to keep with the spirit of Thompson's repertoire selections by including an assortment of treasured pieces that are taught often and hold status as prized concert music. For example, in the 5th Grade volume are two of the most recognized C-sharp Minor pieces in existence: Beethoven's "Moonlight" sonata and the Rachmaninoff prelude, loved and adored with good reason, yet sometimes unfairly disparaged because of their popularity. (Note that this edition presents the often overwhelming final section of the Rachmaninoff in a more visually accessible layout.) In the same book is Debussy's fast, witty "Doctor Gradus ad Parnassum" and Mozart's D Minor fantasy, unfinished at the time of his death and completed by his student August Eberhard Müller. (Müller's "Lyric Etude" is included in the 1st Grade.) Earlier in the series are other oft-cherished pieces, such as Grieg's spare and wistful "Arietta" and Chopin's intense, evolving "Prelude in E Minor" (both in the 4th Grade), as well as several well-known Bartók miniatures from his 1913 method (1st, 2nd, and 3rd Grade books).

Numerous uncommon treasures were also unearthed, including "A Ghost in the Fireplace" (4th Grade) and "Once Upon a Time There was a Princess" (3rd Grade) from Theodor Kullak's *Scenes from Childhood*, composed for piano students well over a century ago. Though these pieces never quite found their way into published recordings or into the hands of master pianists, for years they provided many students with delightful lesson material as they built their pianistic skills. Other lesser-known gems include works from French composers Mélanie Bonis (*Album pour les tout-petits*, 1st and 2nd Grade) and Cécile Chaminade ("Pièce Romantique," 3rd Grade); Danish composer Ludvig Schytte's Opus 108 (1st and 2nd Grade); Russian composer Anatoly Lyadov's gorgeous, seldom-heard B Minor prelude; and English composer Samuel Coleridge-Taylor's mournful "They Will Not Lend Me a Child," based on a Southeast African folksong about a childless mother (both in the 5th Grade). Quick pieces that dazzle and motivate were intentionally included as well; for example, MacDowell's "Alla Tarantella," C.P.E. Bach's "Presto in C Minor" (both in the 3rd Grade), and Moszkowski's "Tarantelle" (4th Grade).

These authentic piano solos are offered once again in these pages, reconnecting the students of today with beautiful masterpieces from bygone eras.

Correlation with John Thompson's Modern Course. The *Classical Piano Solos* series was compiled to correlate loosely with the *Modern Course* method. The series can be used to supplement any teaching method, but holds its own as a small compendium of advancing piano literature. Worth mentioning is that all the pieces are public domain in the United States, Europe, and around the world. Consequently, no works composed or published after 1920 are included. It is highly recommended that the teacher supplement the lesson with appropriate contemporary literature, including works from outside traditional Western art music, as needed.

Leveling and Layout. Grades 1-4 have been presented in a suggested order of study and progress by approximate level of difficulty. Because of the sophistication and advanced technicality of the pieces in Grade 5, that volume is laid out chronologically, from Baroque to the early 20th Century. Page turns were always a consideration during the engraving and editing process.

Editorial Principles and Sources. When appropriate, occasional articulation, fingerings, and dynamics have been added, especially to pieces from the Baroque and early Classical eras, with the intent of better assisting the advancing performer with an accurate stylistic interpretation. (An exception are fingerings in the Bartók pieces; a few were removed for ease of study.) Urtext sources were consulted whenever available, as well as standard performing editions. The first two pieces in the 1st Grade have been slightly adapted; all other works in the series are originals composed for the keyboard/piano of the time. Compositions without designated titles have been bestowed with fresh ones.

CONTENTS

[Suggested order of study; however, it is recommended that two contrasting works be learned concurrently]

Little Waltz

from *The Young Pianist's First Steps,* Op. 82, No. 18

ADAPTED
Cornelius Gurlitt
1820–1901

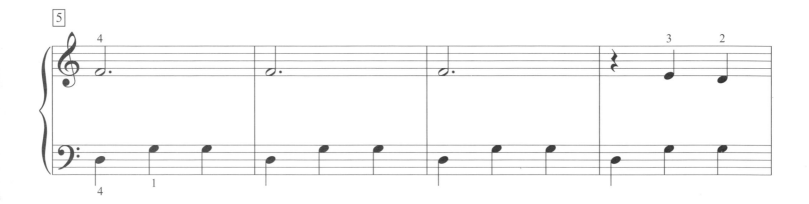

Raindrops

ADAPTED
Jacob Schmitt
1803–1853

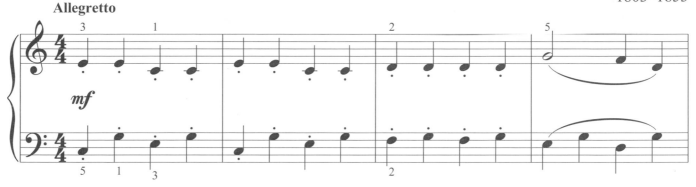

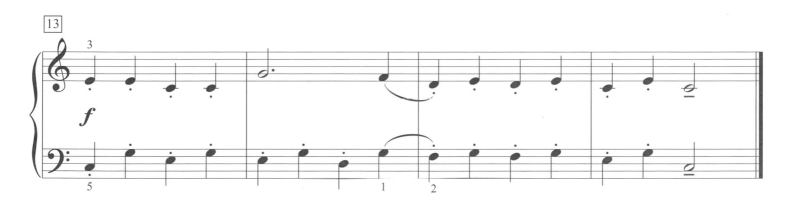

Bravery

from *Handstücke*

Daniel Gottlob Türk
1750–1813

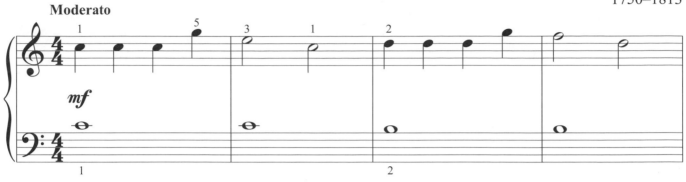

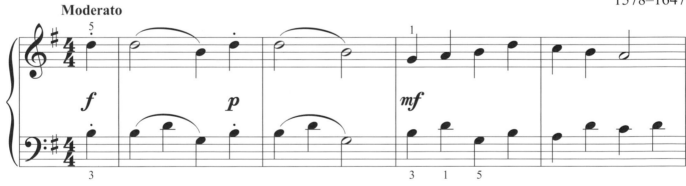

Echo Dance

Philipp Hainhofer
1578–1647

A Conversation

Béla Bartók
1881–1945

Circle Song

Béla Bartók
1881–1945

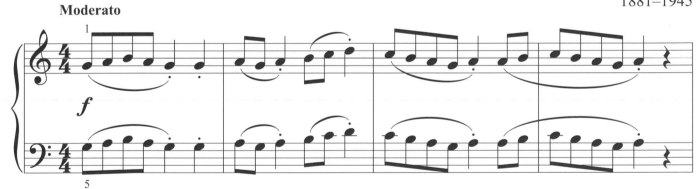

Rustic Dance

Béla Bartók
1881–1945

Moderato

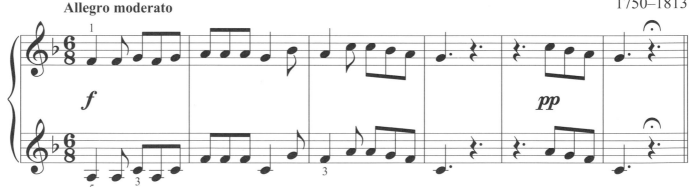

The Echoing Castle
from *Handstücke*

Daniel Gottlob Türk
1750–1813

Allegro moderato

Little Invention

Jakub Jan Ryba
1765–1815

I Feel So Sick and Faint

Daniel Gottlob Türk
1750–1813

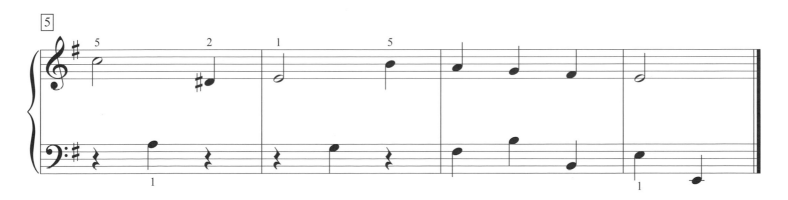

Copycat

Béla Bartók
1881–1945

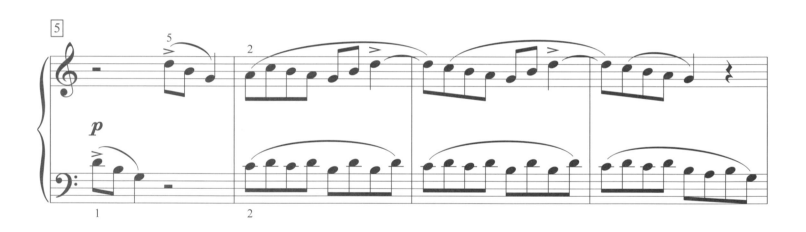

Market Dance

from *Practical Method for the Pianoforte,* Op. 249, No. 27

Louis Köhler
1820–1886

Choral Etude

from *25 Melodious Studies,* Op. 108, No. 3

Ludvig Schytte
1848–1909

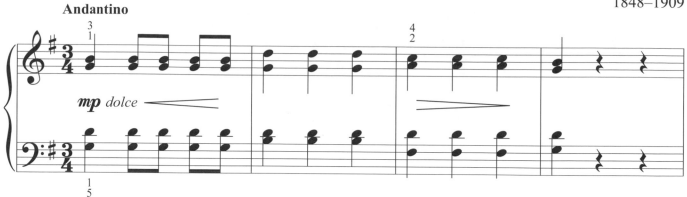

Andantino

Op. 190, No. 27

Louis Köhler
1820–1886

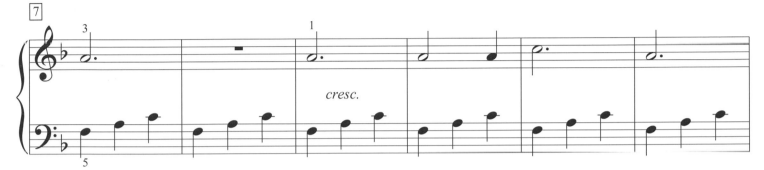

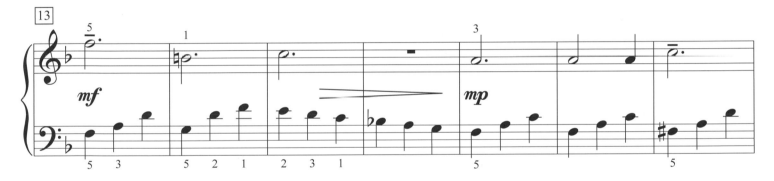

Innocence

from *Handstücke*

Daniel Gottlob Türk
1756–1813

Two-Finger Partita

from *Pour les enfants de tout âge,* Op. 74, No. 1/I.

Vincent d'Indy
1851–1931

[Use only the first two fingers of each hand.]

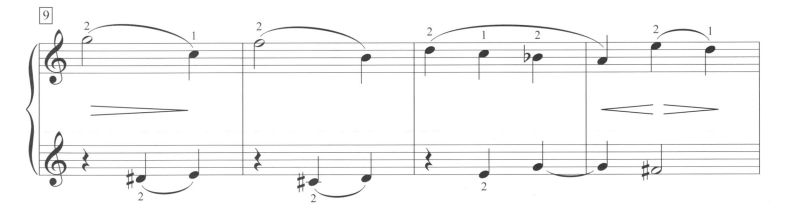

Miaou! Ronron!

from *Album pour les tout-petits*, Op. 103

Mélanie Bonis
1858–1937

Mireille
from *Album pour les tout-petits,* Op. 103

Mélanie Bonis
1858–1937

Springtime

from *25 Melodious Studies,* Op. 108, No. 10

Ludvig Schytte
1848–1909

Passepied in C Major

HWV 559

George Frideric Handel
1685–1759

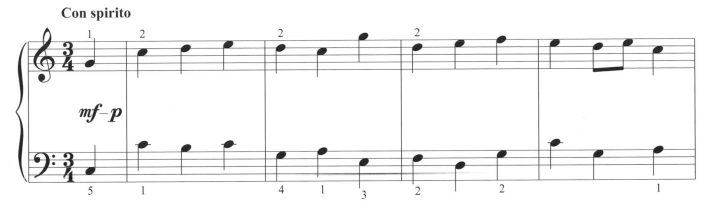

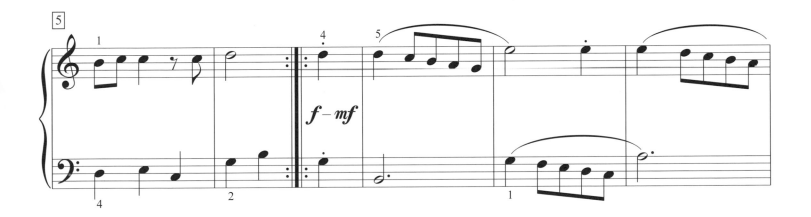

Play quarter notes slightly detached.

Lyric Etude

from *12 Leichte Handstücke,* No. 3

August Eberhard Müller
1767–1817

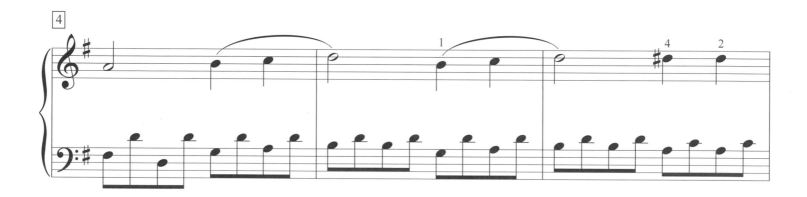

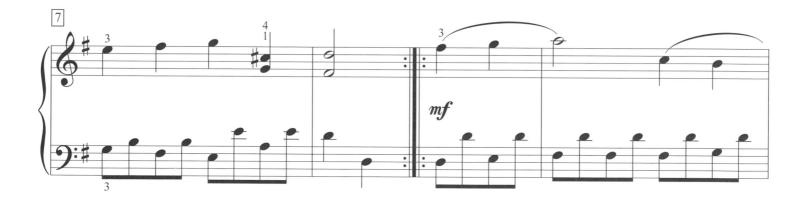

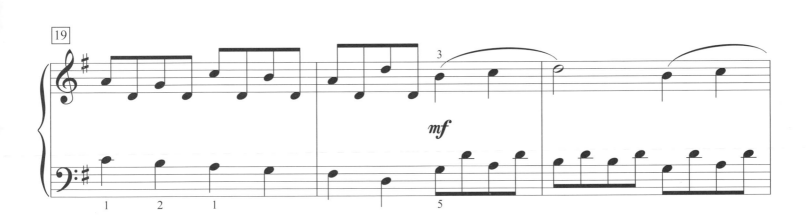

Arabesque

from *25 Progressive Etudes,* Op. 100, No. 2

Friedrich Burgmüller
1806–1874

Allegro scherzando

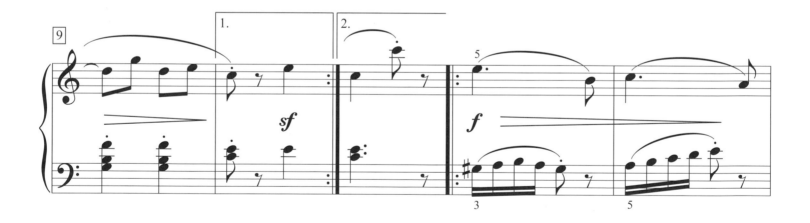

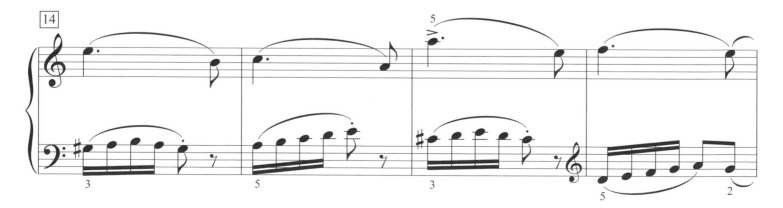

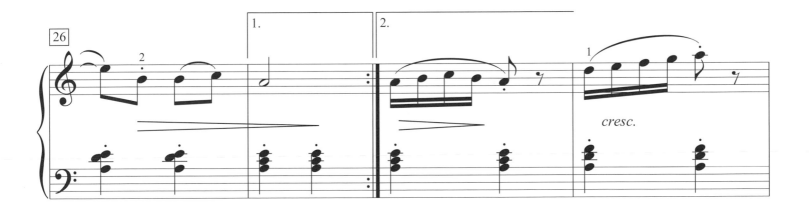

Style characteristics and adjectives that may be helpful when teaching Western keyboard classical music:

BAROQUE (c. 1600-1750) – ornamented, verbose, grand, delicate, decorative, propulsive, embellished, improvisatory, speech-like inflections, counterpoint, binary form, motoric rhythms, drive to the last note of a phrase, the idea of "affections" (each piece has single mood/character).
Major Keyboard Composers: Bach, Handel, Rameau, Scarlatti.

CLASSICAL (c. 1750-1820) – simple, elegant, graceful, natural, melodic, pure, precise, balanced, homophonic (melody with accompaniment), Alberti bass, sonata form, tapered phrases, symmetrical phrases, motivic development, contrasting moods, grace notes played on the beat.
Major Keyboard Composers: Beethoven, Haydn, Mozart.

ROMANTIC (c. 1800-1910) – emotional, dramatic, melodic, *sturm und drang*, flexible, expressive, personal, chromatic, virtuosic, forlorn, nationalistic, programmatic, singing melodies, long gestures, wide leaps, modulations to remote keys, character pieces.
Major Keyboard Composers: Brahms, Chopin, Grieg, Liszt, Mendelssohn, Rachmaninoff, Schumann, Scriabin.

IMPRESSIONIST (c. 1875-1925) – blurry, hazy, misty, colorful, ambiguous (tonality), evocative, parallel chords (planing), pentatonic and whole-tone scales, irregular meter, small/repeated motives and phrases, poetry, painting, nature, mood over clarity, extreme ranges of pitch and dynamics.
Major Keyboard Composers: Debussy, Ravel.

20th CENTURY / CONTEMPORARY (c. 1900-present) – experimental, percussive, complex, electronic, dissonant, atonal, asymmetrical rhythms, changing meters, twelve-tone, serialism, eclectic, diverse formal structures, specific performing directions, individual, folk melodies, global influences.
Major Keyboard Composers: Bartók, Prokofiev.

PHILIP LOW is a piano teacher in Arden Hills, Minnesota, where he maintains a private studio of nearly 50 students. His students have won numerous competitions, including the MMTA state, Young Artist, Northstar Concerto, Piano Fun, and Saint Paul Piano Teachers contests. An active member of MMTA, Dr. Low has volunteered on the convention committee, exam syllabus committee, and foundation board. He has given lectures at the state convention as well as to local music teacher groups. He holds a Masters and Doctorate in piano performance from the Cleveland Institute of Music as well as a Bachelor of Music from Bethel University in St. Paul.

SONYA SCHUMANN received her D.M.A. and M.M. in piano performance and pedagogy from the University of Michigan and a B.M. from the University of South Carolina. She has performed throughout the United States, Canada, Europe, and Australia, and with orchestras across North America, winning top prizes in several competitions. Active in the artistic community, she also serves as an ambassador for the Piano Arts Consortium, performing benefit concerts and giving masterclasses across the East Coast. She has appeared as guest lecturer and masterclass presenter at several festivals and colleges, including Keys Fest, Music Teachers National Association, Central Michigan University, Red Rocks Music Festival, and Art at Noon at LexArts. She has served as faculty at Madonna University and Schoolcraft College. Dr. Schumann has been on the Levine Music School faculty since 2015, teaching group piano classes and private piano.

CHARMAINE SIAGIAN is editor of Willis publications at Hal Leonard Corporation. She received her D.M.A. in piano performance and pedagogy from the University of Oklahoma and her B.M. and M.M. in piano performance from the Dana School of Music at Youngstown State University. Dr. Siagian has served on the piano faculties of Youngstown State University and Mid-America Christian University, teaching classes in applied and group piano, music theory and history, as well as accompanying chamber choirs, musical theater, and opera workshops. Growing up on North Borneo, her first piano book—perhaps fortuitously—was by John Thompson.